Heinemann Library
Chicago, Illinois

Mapping the World

Ana Deboo

Customer Service 888-454-2279

Visit our website at www.heinemannlibrary.com

Designed by David Poole and Geoff Ward
Illustrations by International Mapping (www.internationalmapping.com)
Photo research by Alan Gottlieb and Tracy Cummins
Originated by Modern Age
Printed and bound in China by WKT

08 07 06
10 9 8 7 6 5 4 3 2 1

Library of Congress Cataloging-in-Publication Data
Deboo, Ana.
  Mapping the world / Ana Deboo.
      p. cm. -- (Map readers)
  Includes bibliographical references and index.
  ISBN 1-4034-6789-7 (hc) -- ISBN 1-4034-6796-X (pb)
  1. Cartography--Juvenile literature. I. Title. II. Series.
  GA105.6.D43 2007
  526--dc22

                                  2006003431

13 digit isbn hardback: 978-1-4034-6789-8
13 digit isbn paperback: 978-1-4034-6796-6

Acknowledgments
The author and publisher are grateful to the following for permission to reproduce copyright material: Erich Lessing/ Art Resource, NY p. **16**; Map Division, New York Public Library, Astor, Lenox and Tilden Foundations pp. **5, 24**; Mountain High Maps/Digital Wisdom pp. **4, 14**; North Wind Picture Archives p. **25**; Stockbyte / Superstock p. **12**.

Cover illustration by International Mapping.
Compass image reproduced with permission of Silvia Bukovacc/Shutterstock.

Every effort has been made to contact copyright holders of any material reproduced in this book. Any omissions will be rectified in subsequent printings if notice is given to the publishers.

Special thanks to Daniel Block for his help in the production of this book.

Table of Contents

Some words are shown in bold, **like this**. You can find out what they mean by looking in the glossary.

Introduction

What are maps for? You might be surprised at how many answers there are to that question. A very common answer, of course, is to help you get places. Maps can show you the way when you are lost. Or they can keep you from getting lost in the first place. But planning a journey is just one reason to use a map. You can use maps to learn all kinds of information.

It is important to use the right map for your purpose. Are you taking a long car trip? You need a road map. Planning to take the bus to your friend's house? There is a special map for that, too. If you want to know more about the stars and planets, you can consult an astronomical map. If you want to know more about the natural features of a place—the mountains and rivers and so forth—you should look at a physical map. Some maps show what the weather conditions are or predict what they will be later. There are even maps that show the ocean floor and the directions the currents flow in the water.

Political map.

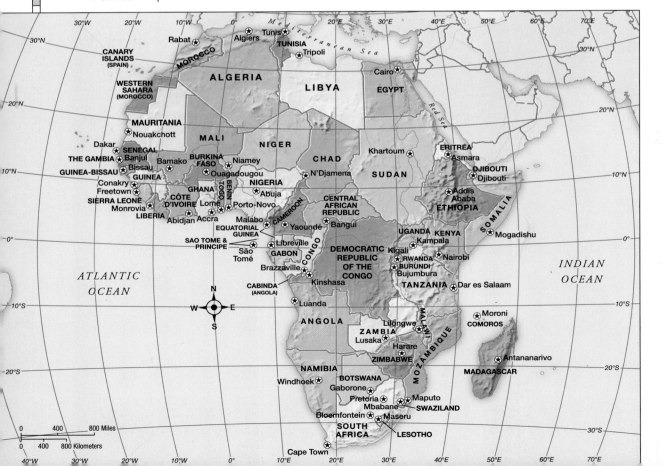

In this book, you will learn about maps that show how and where people live around the world. Political maps show how people have divided and named the land. Borders of regions like states and countries are shown, along with the names of those regions and of the cities and towns within them. Resource and product maps give information about the **economy** of an area. They tell what resources are available there and what people make with those resources. Time zone maps show the borders where time changes in different parts of the world, and population density maps show the number of people living in different areas.

You will also take a look at some historical maps. These will give you an idea of what **cartographers** (mapmakers) used to think the world looked like. They will also show you how borders and names of places change over time. Historical maps can also be made today to show how boundaries have changed.

It is amazing to think of all the things you can learn from maps!

Historical map.

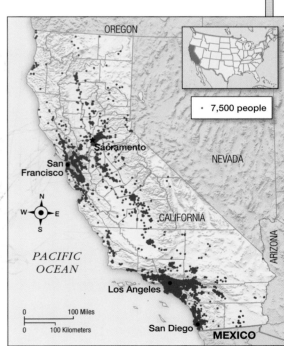

Population density map.

Maps can show many different types of information. These are some of the maps you will learn about in this book.

Reading Maps

There are many different types of maps, but there are certain features nearly all of them have in common. If you learn how to recognize and use these features, you will be prepared to read any map you need.

When looking at a map, you should first read the **map title**. Just like the title of a book or article, it will be in a place you cannot miss, usually at the top. The map title will tell you what the map is about, or what it shows. This will include both the **geographic** area and other specific information about the map, such as the date of the data shown, or the date the map was completed.

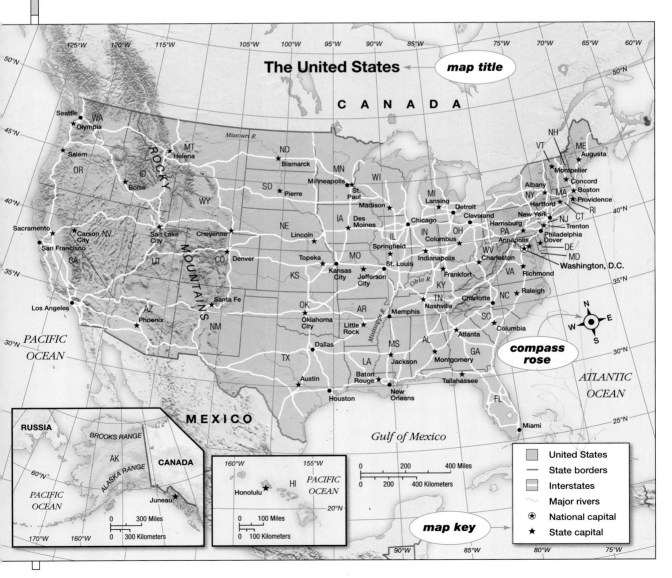

You will also need to find direction on your map. The **compass rose** is a small diagram on a map that confirms the **cardinal directions**: north, south, east, and west.

Next, take a look at the **map key**, or legend. This is a box off to the side that contains all the different symbols used in the map and explains what they stand for. There are several different kinds of symbols. There might be little pictures that are easy to interpret—like a tiny teepee that stands for a campground. There might also be symbols you cannot figure out so easily. For example, different dots could be used to stand for types of cities: a star might indicate a state capital, a large black dot could mark a major city, and a small black dot, a smaller city or town. Color coding is another kind of symbolism you will find in the key. If different colors are used to fill in areas on the map or symbols are shown in more than one color, the key will tell you what they mean.

The key will also tell you about the lines that make up the map. Mapmakers use different colors and thicknesses of lines and dotted or dashed lines in many ways. The various areas shown on the map—countries and states, for example—will all be surrounded by special kinds of lines. On some maps, various types of roads will be shown using a different line depending on the type of road. Blue lines on a map are usually rivers and streams, but check the map key to make sure. The symbols change from map to map.

This is a large-scale map of downtown Atlanta, Georgia.

How much land does your map cover? To figure that out, you need to pay attention to the map's **scale,** or the relationship between the picture on your map and size of the real place. Scale is the number of miles in the real world that fit into each inch on the map (or the kilometers represented by each centimeter, if it is a metric map). You can find out the scale of your map by looking for the **scale bar**, a diagram that looks a little like a ruler. There may also be a sentence below the bar that expresses the scale in words—for example, "20 miles per inch."

Remember that most maps are made from a bird's-eye view, as if the picture was drawn by someone flying directly overhead. Think about how when you are close to something it looks bigger, and when you are farther away from it, it looks smaller. Maps that give a close-up view of a place are called large-scale maps. The details on them are larger than on maps drawn from a higher point of view. Large-scale maps cannot cover a very wide area, though, unless they are printed on a really, really big piece of paper.

A map that shows a wide area but has fewer or smaller details is known as a small-scale map. It gives you the point of view you would have if you were flying high above the land.

Some maps also include a **locator** to show how the map fits into the surrounding area. The locator is a very small-scale **inset map** of that surrounding area with a box on it showing exactly where the main map area is located.

This map shows Atlanta on a smaller scale than the street map on page 8. It shows only the major roads.

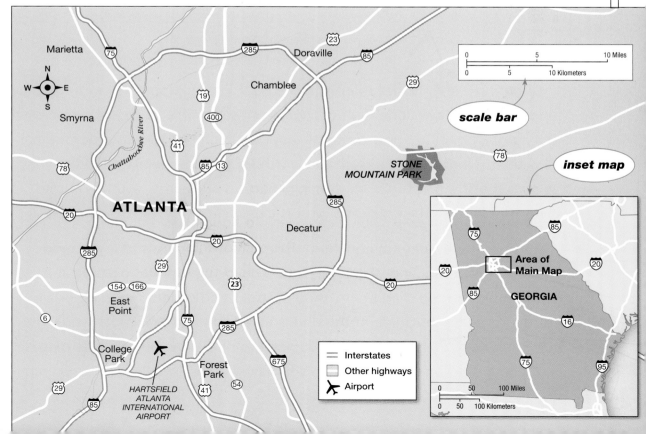

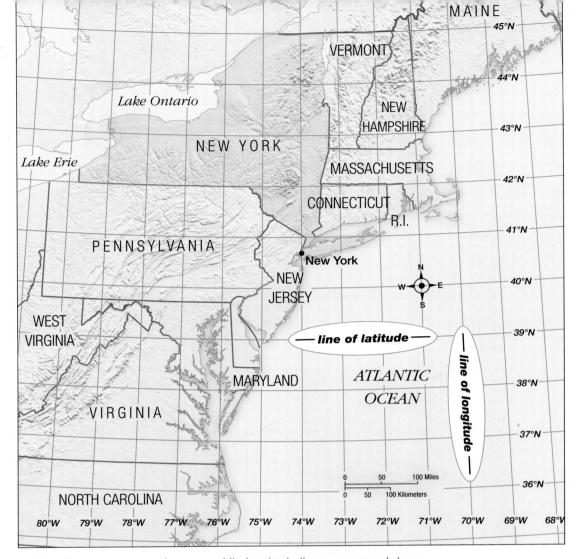

Latitude lines run across the map, while longitude lines run up and down.

Choosing the right size map with the right information on it is important. And once you have done that, you will want to be able to describe places on the map. One of the most common ways of doing this is to use the cardinal directions. North points toward the North Pole. South points the other way, toward the South Pole. On most maps, north is at the top, south is at the bottom, east is to the right, and west is to the left.

Another way of describing where things are on a map is to use a **grid system**, horizontal and vertical lines that divide a map into squares. It is common for a road map or city map to use a grid system made especially for that map. Each square of the grid is assigned an identification code based on its row and column. If you need to find something on the map and you know what square it is in, you have a much smaller area to search than if you had to scan the whole map.

There is also a grid system that is the same for every map. No matter what map you use, you will identify the spot the same way. This is called **absolute location**. The lines in this system have special names: **latitude** and **longitude** lines. Latitude lines, which are also known as parallels, are the horizontal lines. They form circles around the globe and do not ever touch one another. The middle latitude line, the one that circles the fattest part of the Earth, is called the **equator**. Longitude lines, or meridians, are vertical and meet at the North and South Poles.

Latitude lines tell how far north or south a place is from the equator. Longitude lines measure the distance east or west from the **Prime Meridian**, a longitude line that passes through Greenwich, a part of London, England. The locations are expressed in units called **degrees**. You identify a place's location by naming both its latitude and longitude.

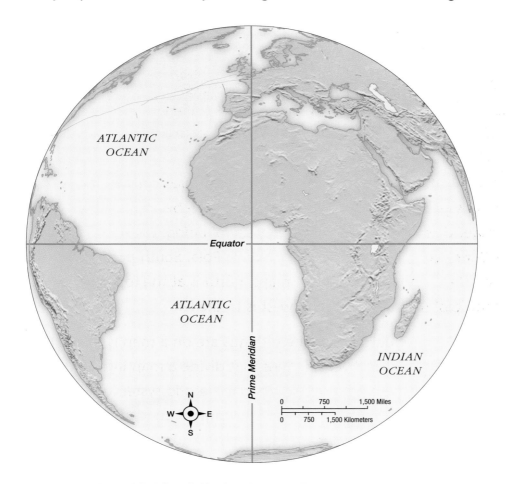

The equator and the Prime Meridian divide the globe into four sections.

Getting to Know Your Globe

Maps can give you a good sense of how parts of the world look, but they have limitations because the Earth is round like a ball. In order to make a flat picture of the round Earth, certain parts have to be stretched so that they are no longer their original size. A globe is a model of the Earth and is the most accurate way of showing what it looks like.

In order to talk about large general areas of the Earth, geographers have divided it in half crosswise and half lengthwise, creating four sections. They call these sections **hemispheres**. Hemisphere means half of a sphere, or ball.

equator

The equator divides the world into the Northern Hemisphere (everything above the equator) and the Southern Hemisphere (everything below the equator).

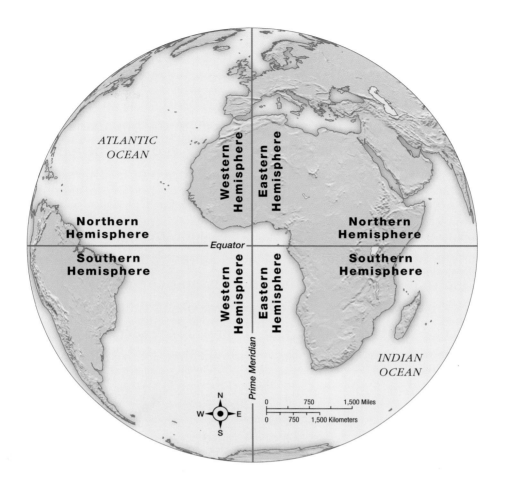

The Northern Hemisphere is the half of the Earth that is north of the equator. The continents of Asia, North America, and Europe are all in the Northern Hemisphere. So are more than half of Africa and a little bit of South America. Most of the people in the world live in this hemisphere. South of the equator is the Southern Hemisphere. It contains South America, Antarctica, Australia, and the lower portion of Africa.

For geographers, the Eastern and Western Hemispheres are separated by the Prime Meridian and the 180° meridian, which form a circle around the Earth through both poles. However, the terms "Eastern Hemisphere" and "Western Hemisphere" are often used by historians in a different way. In this sense, the Eastern Hemisphere is the "Old World," Europe and Asia and Africa. The Western Hemisphere is the "New World" of the Americas, which began to be explored and settled by people from the Old World starting in the 1400s. In the historical sense, the Prime and 180° meridians are not quite the right dividing line between the hemispheres because so much of Europe falls into the Western Hemisphere.

Political Maps

Politics is the practice of government—the ways that groups of people create systems to help them live together and with other groups. A **political map** describes cultural features such as the boundaries and locations of nations, countries, states, provinces, and other man-made divisions. It shows all kinds of place names and boundaries that separate groups of people and their control over different areas.

Political maps sometimes use color to highlight the major areas on the map. For example, the states in the United States or the countries in Africa may be shown in many colors. There is no symbolic meaning to the colors. The cartographer just makes sure that no two places that share a border are the same color. That way it is easy to see how all the different parts of the region fit together and tell one place from another.

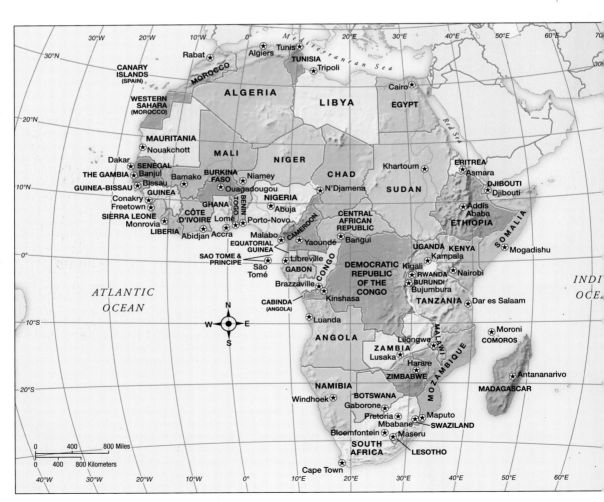

Political map of Africa.

Political maps often include at least some physical features like mountains, lakes, and rivers. That makes it easier for the reader to recognize the place shown. Natural features of the land can also play an important role when people are deciding what the boundaries of a place will be. That is because they make good natural dividing lines. Take a look at a map of the world. How many borders are found along the course of a river? In the United States, for example, the Mississippi River defines at least part of the borders of ten states.

One of the main reasons people consult political maps is to learn where places are and how the different areas on them relate to one another. There is probably a political map of the United States hanging in your classroom at school right now!

Political Divisions

The most common political divisions in the United States are:

- *the country—the whole region,*
- *states—smaller regions within the country,*
- *counties—divisions within states, and*
- *cities—areas within a region (or county) where many people live.*

There are similar political divisions around the world, although they may have different names and functions. For example, Canada is made up of provinces rather than states. And many of the countries in Europe joined together to create a new and larger political unit, the European Union, in 1993.

Time Zone Maps

Less than 200 years ago, time was not something everybody agreed on. There were clocks, but people set them according to their best guess of the time, usually based on the Sun's position. In towns, people followed their church clock because everyone could see it. But one town's church clock might say something different than the church clock in the town ten miles down the road. Then in the 1800s, the railroads became popular. How can you make a train schedule if the clocks in the places where the train stops all have a different time? So it was decided that everybody would use the same system for setting clocks.

Of course, the whole world cannot use the exact same time. When the Sun shines on one side of the Earth, making it daytime, it is dark— nighttime—on the other side. Around 1869, an American educator named Charles Dowd thought of a solution to that problem. He suggested dividing the Earth into four vertical time zones. Dowd began traveling around, trying to gain support for his plan.

Before the mid-1900s, most people did not have watches. Clock towers were an important way to tell time, and were usually placed in the center of town.

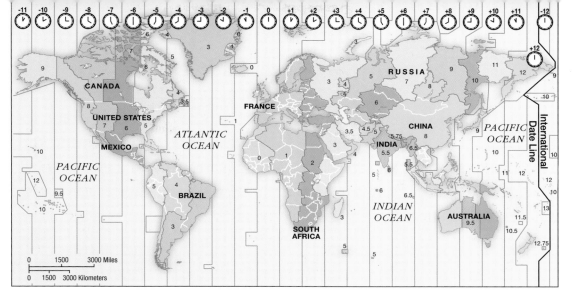

The lines that divide time zones are fairly straight. They curve around things like islands to keep them in the same time zone as the country of which they are a part.

Sir Sandford Fleming, a retired railway engineer in Canada, also wanted to solve the time problem. He divided the Earth lengthwise (north to south) into 24 zones, one for each hour of the day. In each zone, the time would be one hour earlier than the zone directly to the east. Thanks in large part to Fleming's work, an international time conference was held in Washington, D.C., in 1884. There, representatives from around the world agreed to use Fleming's system.

A **time zone** map shows where the zones begin and end using either lines or color-coding. The dividing lines are based on longitude lines, but they are not always straight. Sometimes they zigzag to follow borders or avoid creating awkward time differences—for example, by crossing through a city. On most world time zone maps, the Prime Meridian in Greenwich, England is at the center. The time at this longitude is known as Universal Time or Greenwich Mean Time. Whenever people in different parts of the world need to use a standard time, they use Universal Time.

The International Date Line
Another line you will find on time zone maps is the International Date Line. This line follows the 180° longitude line, occasionally swerving off the line to avoid separating countries into two dates. It is where the date begins and ends. Any time of day, if you cross the line toward the west it becomes a day later, and if you cross the line toward the east it becomes a day earlier.

Thematic Maps Overview

A thematic map gives information about a particular subject or theme. These maps have many uses, such as showing what products are made in a location or how many people live in a certain area. They are especially intended to help you compare information about the different places on the map.

Thematic maps begin with a **base map**, or simplified map of a place. The base map will show the outline of the place, as well as details like city names, if they are needed. The factual information is then layered on top of the base map. There are several ways of using colors, symbols, shapes, lines, or some combination of these elements to show information. Whatever the method, the map key will help you understand what is found on the map.

Source: U.S. Census

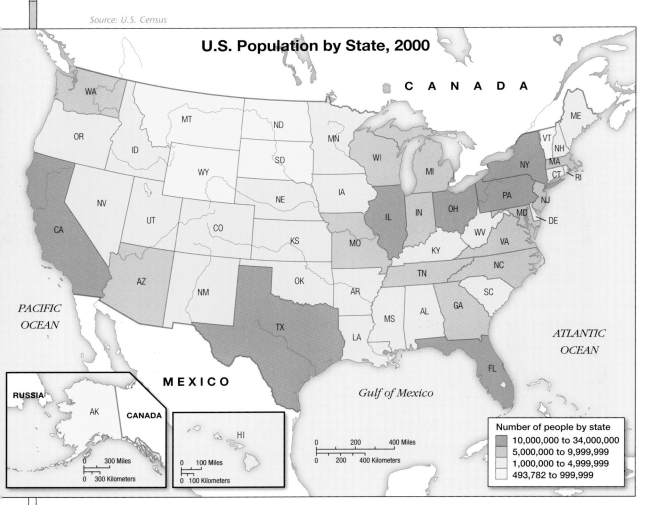

U.S. Population by State, 2000

Number of people by state
- 10,000,000 to 34,000,000
- 5,000,000 to 9,999,999
- 1,000,000 to 4,999,999
- 493,782 to 999,999

This map uses color to show the total population per state. Thematic maps such as this one show numeric data.

The information given on thematic maps is usually one of two types. One type shows the amount of something to be found in an area. For example, you could make a map that shows the total U.S. population by state. Looking at the map, you would see at a glance which states have the largest amounts of people and which have the fewest. These types of maps often use different shades of the same color to show the different amounts of something across an area.

2004 U.S. Presidential Election Results

Bush states
Kerry states

This thematic map shows the results of the 2004 presidential election. It does not show the number of votes each candidate got, but it does show which states they won.

The second type of map does not show the exact amount of something in an area. Instead, these maps give other specific types of information. For example, say you wanted to know which states voted for President Bush or John Kerry in the 2004 Presidential Election. You would not need to know the number of votes the candidates got in each state, just the end results. These types of maps often use different colors to show the different types of information.

Some thematic maps even combine these two types. They tell what kinds of things and how many things can be found in the places shown.

Thematic Maps: Economic Maps

Thematic maps are often used to give economic information. For example, there is a type of map called a land use map that can serve many purposes. An **agricultural** land use map might show how much land is used for growing crops and how much is pasture for livestock. You could even make a more detailed map showing what types of crops are grown in an area and what types of animals graze in the pastures.

Someone interested in building houses would look for a different land use map. That person would want a map showing what areas are already covered with housing, what areas have commercial buildings like stores and offices, where there is park land that cannot be built on, and which properties are empty and available. Land use maps are often color-coded, and each land type is assigned a color or pattern.

Resource and product maps focus on—what else?—resources (materials) and products (often called goods and services). Goods are objects you can buy, like cookies or computers. Services are things people are paid to do, like operate the grocery store cash register, bake cookies to sell, or design computers.

Source: USDA, Agricultural Statistic Board, Corn Production Summary

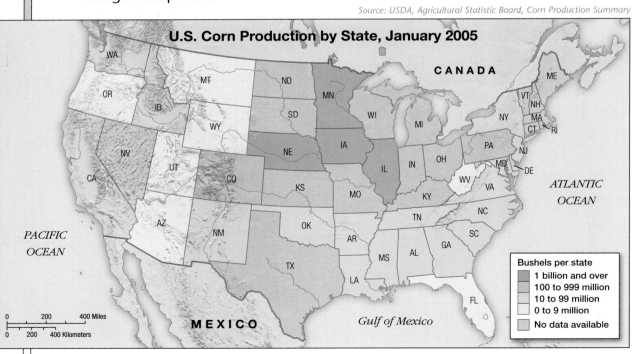

U.S. Corn Production by State, January 2005

Bushels per state
- 1 billion and over
- 100 to 999 million
- 10 to 99 million
- 0 to 9 million
- No data available

This map shows corn production by state. Darker colors often represent larger amounts of something on maps, but always check the map key to be sure.

An agricultural land use map that shows crops and livestock could be considered a resource and product map. Another type of resource map might show natural resources, such as the types of valuable minerals and metals in the ground. A mining company that was trying to decide where to dig a mine would want that information. Environmentalists who heard about the mining company's plans might look up a different natural resource map of the same area, one showing the plants and animals that live there. They could use that map to try to convince people that mining would endanger the wildlife.

Source: World Bank Development Indicators

Gross Domestic Product Per Person

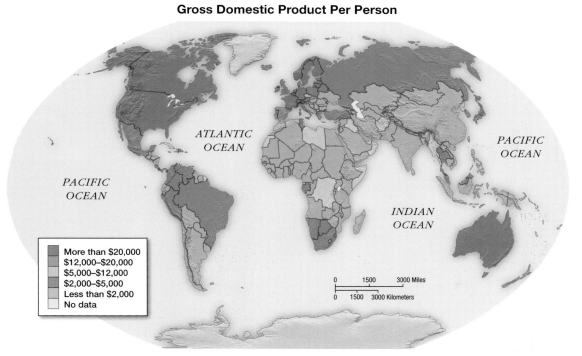

Gross Domestic Product is a way of measuring the economy of an area. It measures things like how many local goods are bought by foreign nations, and how many goods the country buys from foreign nations.

Resource and product maps often use symbols instead of color-coding so they can show more than one type of product or resource. Each symbol can also represent a certain number or amount of something so the map can show even more information. For example, on a map that shows what types of crops are grown in an area, tiny pictures of ears of corn might symbolize where corn is grown, and each symbol might stand for 1,000 bushels. If 2,000 bushels of corn are produced in one area, then there will be two corn symbols on that part of the map.

Thematic Maps: Population Density

Population density means the number of people who live in a given area, often a square mile or square kilometer. Population density maps are useful because they show where people have settled in the areas on the map—where it is crowded, and where it is not so crowded. You can learn interesting things from these maps. For example, a business might consult a population density map of an area to find out if enough people live within driving distance to make it worth opening a new shop there.

Population density is usually presented either as a color-coded map or as a dot density map. Instead of using several colors, color-coded population density maps often use different shades of one color. The darkest shades represent larger numbers of people, and the lightest are used for places with the fewest people. In dot density maps, each dot represents a certain number of people, and the dots are clustered in areas of higher population.

Source: USDA, NRCS

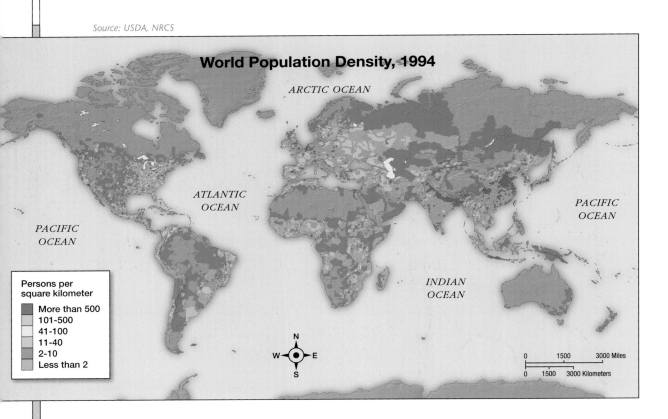

World Population Density, 1994

Persons per square kilometer

- More than 500
- 101-500
- 41-100
- 11-40
- 2-10
- Less than 2

Source: US Census, 2004

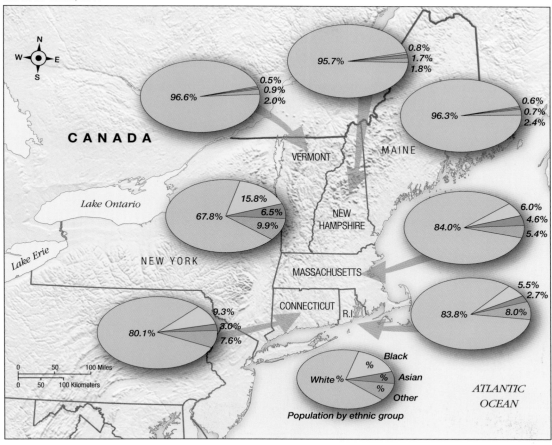

These pie charts shows the racial makeup of New England by state.

There are other thematic maps that represent the groups of people who live in an area. Maps with an **ethnographic** focus give you a general sense of the race or culture of the people who live in the areas shown. For example, one map might show the territories of the tribes of Native Americans during colonial times. Another might show the racial groups that live in the United States now.

Ethnographic maps may be color-coded, but they can also be presented as chart maps, with a chart (such as a pie chart or a bar graph) to represent focus areas. Pie charts would be a good choice for a map of the racial make-up of the United States. For each state, a pie chart would indicate the percentage of the state's total population who are of European, African, Hispanic, Middle Eastern, or Asian descent, as well as other heritages.

Historical Maps

Maps have been around for a long time. Whenever people have needed to find their way or define boundaries, they have usually drawn a map. Archaeologists have dug up clay tablet maps at the site of the ancient city of Babylon. Some of these tablets are more than 4,000 years old!

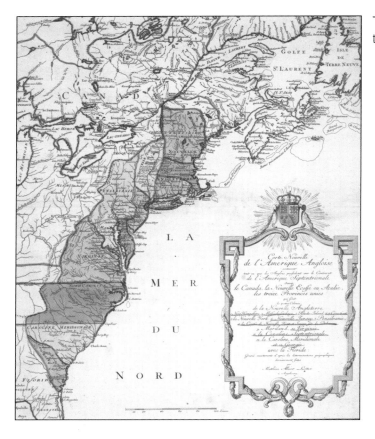

This historical map shows the original 13 colonies.

Looking at **historical maps**, we can learn what places used to be like and how they have changed over time. For example, when people began mapping the United States, they had not yet ventured very far from the East Coast. But the territory grew steadily, and historical maps document the settler's progress. The original 13 English colonies eventually became U.S. states. In 1803, the Louisiana Purchase doubled the size of the country by adding more than 800,000 square miles of new territory, part of which is now known as Louisiana. For years borders shifted, the territory expanded, and names changed. The United States we are familiar with today did not exist until well into the 20th century. Alaska and Hawaii, the 49th and 50th states, did not join the country until 1959.

THE UNITED STATES in 1792

The Mississippi was then the western boundary of the United States, but we had a claim on the Oregon country. (See above). England, Spain and Russia also claimed Oregon.

SCALE OF MILES
0 50 100   200   300   400   500

With the Louisiana Purchase, the United States gained nearly 530 million acres of land.

The term "historical map" does not just refer to maps that are very old. Things keep changing in the world, and any map with out-of-date information is historical. In 2003, Yugoslavia, an Eastern European country, decided to change its name to Serbia and Montenegro. This meant that maps of the area had to be updated. All the earlier maps became historical documents even though they were not very old. Now they are interesting because they show how things were before.

Historical maps can also be new maps made about historical topics. For example, a cartographer could make a modern set of maps showing the changing boundaries of Eastern Europe.

Terra Incognita

Before modern technology made precise mapping possible, people made maps by documenting what they saw when they traveled. Sometimes cartographers decided to include places they had only heard about. The problem was that there were some outlandish rumors circulating about those far-off places. On a few historical maps, you will find imaginary islands or pictures of strange beings in unknown land and waters (which, in Latin, was called "terra incognita").

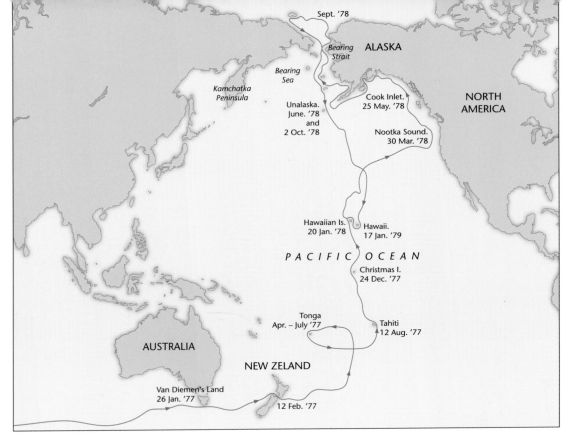

This map shows the route Captain James Cook followed on one of his expeditions in the Pacific Ocean.

Another fascinating kind of historical map is the route map. Whenever past explorers set out on a journey, they made maps. This not only helped them to get back home, but it documented what they had discovered. In the early days of mapmaking, information gathered by explorers was very helpful to cartographers who wanted to fill in the gaps on their maps of the world. A route map is a kind of thematic map; it gives information about where someone went. It includes a base map of the area explored and has a line showing the path the explorers followed. Usually the line includes arrowheads to indicate the direction in which they traveled.

One explorer who made impressive maps of his journeys was Captain James Cook. Between 1759 and 1779, Cook explored Canada and made three expeditions to learn about the Pacific Ocean. On each expedition, he took along a team of scientists to collect information about plants and animals in the new lands, as well as to work on navigational matters such as how to determine longitude lines accurately. Cook and his team mapped the coasts of many countries. Often they were the first Europeans to see the lands they charted, such as the Hawaiian islands. A route map of Captain Cook's journeys shows just how impressive his achievement was.

Scholars can use old historical maps to make a new map with historical information on it. For example, to show a country's shifting borders, they might draw the older border as a dotted line on a base map of the modern country. Or they might use a new physical map as a base map to show the route of a long-ago explorer. These kinds of maps allow historians to combine what we know now about the world with what happened in the past.

Source: CIA

These maps show the political boundaries of Eastern Europe in 1985 (left) and 2005. Even though it was newly drawn, the map on the left is a historical map because it shows old boundaries.

As you can see, people have used maps to represent information about the world for a very long time. Nearly any information about a place can be presented on a map. And only a little basic background knowledge is usually needed to understand the information at a glance. Now that you have that background knowledge, keep an eye out for maps. You will notice them in all kinds of places.

Map Activities

Try making a thematic map of your town showing the places that are important in your life. Start by drawing a base map of the area. Think of areas like parks, your school, your home, friends' homes, and stores. Create a color code to identify each of these. Create symbols for places you like to go. For instance, show where you can get ice cream, play basketball, or see a movie. Color in the areas and place the symbols in the right spots. Don't forget to include a legend and a compass rose, and give your map a title!

Now that you are familiar with some of the ways we map our world, maybe you can try some of these ideas, too:

- Try comparing a population density map to a map of the same area that shows physical and political details. Notice that you can see how the natural features influence where people settle. Very few people live in deserts (like the Sahara Desert) or in very cold places (like Siberia). People do cluster along rivers and coasts, though. There are often cities (and high densities of people) at the places where rivers cross or flow into an ocean. Historically, those spots have been the best places for trading goods, so cities were established there.

- Make a population density map for the houses in your neighborhood. Draw a base map that shows the houses on your street. In each house, put a dot for every person who lives there. If you like, you can color-code the dots to show different members of your family—even dogs and cats.

- If you live in a city, look for an old tourist map of it at the library. Can you find things that have changed since that historical map was printed? If you live in a rural area, look for a historical map of your county or an old state map.

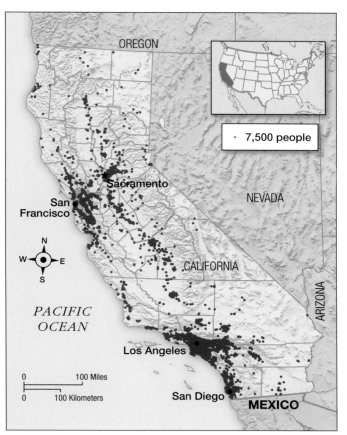

OREGON

7,500 people

Sacramento

San
Francisco

NEVADA

N
W—E
S

CALIFORNIA

ARIZONA

PACIFIC
OCEAN

Los Angeles

0   100 Miles

0   100 Kilometers

San Diego

MEXICO

Compare the population density map and physical map of California, left and below. On the physical map, brown represents dry, desert areas, and mountainous areas appear bumpy. How do you think the natural features of the state have affected where people live?

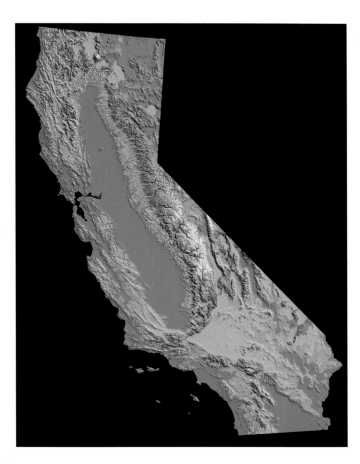

Glossary

absolute location location of a spot on Earth determined by a standard system, such as latitude and longitude

agricultural related to farming

base map background map showing the geographic area covered by a thematic map. The thematic information—population density, routes, and the like—is layered on top of the base map.

cardinal direction one of the four main directions including north, south, east, and west

cartographer mapmaker

compass rose diagram on a chart or map that shows direction

degree unit of latitude or longitude used to locate places on Earth

economy production and use of goods and services in a certain area

equator 0° latitude line at the center of the Earth that divides the Northern Hemisphere from the Southern Hemisphere

ethnographic related to the study of different peoples' cultures

geographic related to geography, the study of the Earth's surface

grid system system that divides the map into smaller squares using horizontal and vertical lines so you can find places more easily

hemisphere half of a sphere

historical map map from an earlier time, or a modern-day map that shows how the land looked at an earlier time

inset map smaller map within or to the side of a larger map. Insets usually show a place in more detail or serve as locators.

latitude measure of how far north or south places are on the globe. Latitude lines are imaginary horizontal rings on the globe created by mapmakers to indicate position. Latitude lines are also called parallels.

locator very small-scale inset map within a larger map that shows where the area in the main map fits in with the land around it

longitude measure of how far east or west places are on the globe. Longitude lines are imaginary vertical rings on the globe created by mapmakers to indicate position. Longitude lines are also called meridians.

map key also called legend. A table that shows and explains all symbols, lines, and colors used on the map.

map title name of the map that indicates the area or type of information included

political map map that focuses on the names and boundaries of places

population density number of people who live within an area

Prime Meridian 0° longitude line, which runs through Greenwich in England and serves as the dividing line between the Eastern and Western Hemispheres

scale amount that a map has been reduced from the size of the real place. The scale tells how many real miles are represented by every inch (or centimeter) on the map.

scale bar small, ruler-like drawing on a map that indicates the map's scale

time zone one of the 24 lengthwise divisions on the Earth that has the same time throughout. Each time zone is one hour earlier than the time zone directly to its east.

Further Reading

Bredeson, Carmen. *Looking at Maps and Globes*.
New York: Children's Press, 2002.

Coupe, Robert. *Maps and Our World*.
Broomall, PA: Mason Crest Publishers, 2003.

Oleksy, Walter. *Maps in History*.
London: Scholastic, 2003.

Index

180° meridian, 13

absolute location, 11
agricultural land use maps, 20, 21
astronomical maps, 4

bar graphs, 23
base maps, 18
borders, 5, 14, 15, 27, *27*

cardinal directions, 7, 10
cartographers, 5, 14, 25, 26
chart maps, 23
city maps, 10
color coding, 7, 14, 18, 19, 20, 22, 23
compass rose, 7
Cook, James, 26

dates, 6
degrees, 11
dot density maps, 22
Dowd, Charles, 16

Eastern Hemisphere, 13
economy, 5
election maps, *19*
equator, 11
ethnographic maps, 23, *23*
exploration, 26, *26*, 27

Fleming, Sir Sandford, 17

geographic area, 6
globes, 12, 13–14
Greenwich Mean Time, 17
grid system, 10–11
Gross Domestic Product maps, *21*

hemispheres, 12–13
historical maps, 5, *5*, 24–27, *24*, *25*, *26*, *27*

inset maps, 9
International Date Line, 17

key, 7, 18

land use maps, 20, 21
large-scale maps, 9
latitude, 11, *11*
legend. *See* key.
locators, 9
longitude, 11, *11*, 17
Louisiana Purchase, 24, *25*

map titles, 6
mapmakers. *See* cartographers.
meridians. *See* longitude.

Northern Hemisphere, 13

ocean floor maps, 4

parallels. *See* latitude.
physical maps, 4, 27
pie charts, 23, *23*
place names, 5
political divisions, 15
political maps, *4*, 5, 14–15
population density maps, 5, *18*, 22–23, *22*
Prime Meridian, 11, 13, 17
product maps, 5, 20–21, *21*

resource maps, 5, 20–21, 21
road maps, 4, 10

roads, 7
route maps, 26, *26*, 27

scale, 8
scale bar, 8
Southern Hemisphere, 13
symbols, 7, 18, 21

"terra incognita," 25
thematic maps, 18–19, *18*, *19*, 20–21, *20*, *21*, 22–23, *22*, *23*, 26, *26*
time, 16, *16*
time zone maps, 5, 16–17, *17*

Universal Time, 17

water current maps, 4
weather maps, 4
Western Hemisphere, 13

Italicized numbers indicate illustrations, photographs, or maps.